On the Profit of Believing

On the Profit of Believing

St. Augustine

On the Profit of Believing

© Lighthouse Publishing 2018

Written by: St. Augustine (Nov.13 354 – Aug.28 430)

Translated by: Rev. C. L. Cornish. M.A.

Updated into Modern U.S English by A.M. Overett (b. 1960)

All rights reserved. Without limiting the rights under copyright reserved above, no part of this publication may be reproduced, stored in a retrieval system, or transmitted, in any form or by any means (electronic, mechanical, photocopying, recording or otherwise), without the prior written permission of the copyright owner of this book.

Published by
Lighthouse Christian Publishing
SAN 257-4330
5531 Dufferin Drive
Savage, Minnesota, 55378
United States of America

www.lighthousechristianpublishing.com

Introductory Notice.

Retract. i. cap. 14. Moreover now at Hippo-Regius as Presbyter I wrote a book on the Profit of Believing, to a friend of mine who had been taken in by the Manichees, and whom I knew to be still held in that error, and to deride the Catholic school of Faith, in that men were bid believe, but not taught what was truth by a most certain method. In this book I said, &c. * * *. This book begins thus, "Si mihi Honorate, unum atque idem videretur esse." St. Augustin enumerates his book on the Profit of Believing first amongst those he wrote as Presbyter, to which order he was raised at Hippo about the beginning of the year 391. The person for whom he wrote had been led into error by himself, and appears to have been recovered from it, at least if he is the same who wrote to St. Augustin from Carthage about 412, proposing several questions, and to whom St. Augustin wrote his 140th Epistle. Cassiodorus calls him a Presbyter, though at that time he was not baptized. In Ep. 83, St. Augustin speaks of the death of another Honoratus, a Presbyter. Towards the end of his life he also wrote his 228th Epistle to a Bishop of Thabenna of the same name. — (Bened. Ed.) The remarks in the Retractations are given in notes to the passages where they occur.

1. IF, Honoratus, a heretic, and a man trusting heretics seemed to me one and the same, I should judge it my duty to remain silent both in tongue and pen in this matter. But now, whereas there is a very great difference between these two: forasmuch as he, in my opinion, is a heretic, who, for the sake of some temporal advantage, and chiefly for the sake of his own glory and pre-eminence, either gives birth to, or follows, false and new opinions; but he, who trusts men of this kind, is a man deceived by a certain imagination of truth and piety. This being the case, I have not thought it my duty to be silent towards you, as to my opinions on the finding and retaining of truth: with great love of which, as you know, we have burned from our very earliest youth: but it is a thing far removed from the minds of vain men, who, having too far advanced and fallen into these corporeal things, think that there is nothing else than what they perceive by those five well-known reporters of the body; and what impressions and images they have received from these, they carry over with themselves, even when they essay to withdraw from the senses; and by the deadly and most deceitful rule of these think that they measure most rightly the unspeakable recesses of truth. Nothing is easier, my dearest friend, than for one not only to say, but also to think, that he hath found out the truth; but how difficult it is in reality, you will perceive, I trust, from this letter of mine. And that this may profit you, or at any rate may in no way harm you, and also all, into whose hands it shall chance to come, I have both prayed, and do pray, unto God; and I hope that it will be so, forasmuch as I am fully conscious that I have undertaken to write it, in a pious and friendly spirit, not as aiming at vain reputation, or trifling display.

2. It is then my purpose to prove to you, if I can, that the Manichees profanely and rashly inveigh against those, who, following the authority of the Catholic Faith, before that they are able to gaze upon that Truth, which the pure mind beholds, are by believing forearmed, and prepared for God Who is about to give them light. For you know, Honoratus, that for no other reason we fell in with such men, than because they used to say, that, apart from all terror of authority, by pure and simple reason, they would lead within to God, and set free from all error those who were willing to be their hearers. For what else constrained me, during nearly nine years, spurning the religion which had been set in me from a child by my parents, to be a follower and diligent hearer of those men, save that they said that we are alarmed by superstition, and are commanded to have faith before reason, but that they urge no one to have faith, without having first discussed and made clear the truth? Who would not be enticed by such promises, especially the mind of a young man desirous of the truth, and further a proud and talkative mind by discussions of certain learned men in the school? such as they then found me, disdainful forsooth as of old wives' fables, and desirous to grasp and drink in, what they promised, the open and pure Truth? But what reason, on the other hand, recalled me, not to be altogether joined to them, so that I continued in that rank which they call of Hearers, so that I resigned not the hope and business of this world; save that I noticed that they also are rather eloquent and full in refutation of others, than abide firm and sure in proof of what is their own. But of myself what shall I say, who was already a Catholic Christian? teats which now, after very long thirst, I almost exhausted and dry, have returned to with all greediness,

and with deeper weeping and groaning have shaken together and wrung them out more deeply, that so there might flow what might be enough to refresh me affected as I was, and to bring back hope of life and safety. What then shall I say of myself? You, not yet a Christian, who, through encouragement from me, execrating them greatly as you did, were hardly led to believe that you ought to listen to them and make trial of them, by what else, I pray you, were you delighted, call to mind, I entreat you, save by a certain great presumption and promise of reasons? But because they disputed long and much with very great copiousness and vehemence concerning the errors of unlearned men, a thing which I learned too late at length to be most easy for any moderately educated man; if even of their own they implanted in us anything, we thought that we were obliged to retain it, insomuch as there fell not in our way other things, wherein to acquiesce. So they did in our case what crafty fowlers are wanting to do, who set branches smeared with bird-lime beside water to deceive thirsty birds. For they fill up and cover anyhow the other waters which are around, or fright them from them by alarming devices, that they may fall into their snares, not through choice, but want.

3. But why do I not make answer to myself, that these fair and clever similes, and charges of this nature may be poured forth against all who are teachers of anything by any adversary, with abundance of wit and sarcasm? But I thought that I ought to insert something of this kind in my letter, in order to admonish them to give over such proceedings; so that, as he says, apart from trifles of common-places, matter may contend with matter, cause with cause, reason with reason. Wherefore

let them give over that saying, which they have in their mouths as though of necessity, when anyone, who hath been for some long time a hearer, hath left them; "The Light hath made a passage through him." For you see, you who are my chief care, (for I am not over anxious about them,) how empty this is, and most easy for anyone to find fault with. Therefore I leave this for your own wisdom to consider. For I have no fear that you will think me possessed by indwelling Light, when I was entangled in the life of this world, having a darkened hope, of beauty of wife, of pomp of riches, of emptiness of honors, and of all other hurtful and deadly pleasures. For all these, as is not unknown to you, I ceased not to desire and hope for, at the time when I was their attentive hearer. And I do not lay this to the charge of their teaching; for I also confess that they also carefully advise to shun these. But now to say that I am deserted by light, when I have turned myself from all these shadows of things, and have determined to be content with that diet merely which is necessary for health of body; but that I was enlightened and shining, at a time when I loved these things, and was wrapped up in them, is the part of a man, to use the mildest expression, wanting in a keen insight into matters, on which he loves to speak at length. But, if you please, let us come to the cause in hand.

4. For you well know that the Manichees move the unlearned by finding fault with the Catholic Faith, and chiefly by rending in pieces and tearing the Old Testament: and they are utterly ignorant, how far these things are to be taken, and how drawn out they descend with profit into the veins and marrows of souls as yet as it were but able to cry. And because there are in them

certain things which are some slight offense to minds ignorant and careless of themselves, (and there are very many such,) they admit of being accused in a popular way: but defended in a popular way they cannot be, by any great number of persons, by reason of the mysteries that are contained in them. But the few, who know how to do this, do not love public and much talked of controversies and disputes: and on this account are very little known, save to such as are most earnest in seeking them out. Concerning then this rashness of the Manichees, whereby they find fault with the Old Testament and the Catholic Faith, listen, I entreat you, to the considerations which move me. But I desire and hope that you will receive them in the same spirit in which I say them. For God, unto Whom are known the secrets of my conscience knows, that in this discourse I am doing nothing of evil craft; but, as I think it should be received, for the sake of proving the truth, for which one thing we have now long ago determined to live; and with incredible anxiety, lest it may have been most easy for me to err with you, but most difficult, to use no harder term, to hold the right way with you. But I venture to anticipate that, in this hope, wherein I hope that you will hold with us the way of wisdom, He will not fail me, unto Whom I have been consecrated; Whom day and night I endeavor to gaze upon: and since, by reason of my sins, and by reason of past habit, having the eye of the mind wounded by strokes of feeble opinions, I know that I am without strength, I often entreat with tears, and as, after long blindness and darkness the eyes being hardly opened, and as yet, by frequent throbbing and turning away, refusing the light which yet they long after; specially if one endeavor to show to them the very sun; so it has now befallen me, who do not deny that there is a certain unspeakable and singular good of the soul, which the mind sees; and who with tears and groaning confess that I am not yet worthy of it. He will not then fail me, if I feign nothing, if I am led by duty, if I love truth, if I esteem friendship, if I fear much lest you be deceived.

5. All that Scripture therefore, which is called the Old Testament, is handed down fourfold to them who desire to know it, according to history, according to ætiology, according to analogy, according to allegory. Do not think me silly for using Greek words. In the first place, because I have so received, nor do I dare to make known to you otherwise than I have received. Next you yourself perceive, that we have not in use terms for such things: and had I translated and made such, I should have been indeed sillier: but, were I to use circumlocution, I should be less free in treating: this only I pray you to believe, that in whatever way I err, I am not inflated or swollen in any thing that I do. Thus (for example) it is handed down according to history, when there is taught what hath been written, or what hath been done; what not done, but only written as though it had been done. According to ætiology, when it is shown for what cause any thing hath been done or said. According to analogy, when it is shown that the two Testaments, the Old and the New, are not contrary the one to the other. According to allegory, when it is taught that certain things which have been written are not to be taken in the letter, but are to be understood in a figure.

6. All these ways our Lord Jesus Christ and His Apostles used. For when it had been objected that His

disciples had plucked the ears of corn on the sabbath-day, the instance was taken from history; "Have ye not read," says He, "what David did when he was an hungered, and they that were with him; how he entered into the house of God, and did eat the shewbread, which was not lawful for him to eat, neither for them that were with him, but only for the priests?" But the instance pertains to ætiology, that, when Christ had forbidden a wife to be put away, save for the cause of fornication, and they, who asked Him, had alleged that Moses had granted permission after a writing of divorcement had been given, This, says He, "Moses did because of the hardness of your heart." For here a reason was given, why that had been well allowed by Moses for a time; that this command of Christ might seem to show that now the times were other. But it were long to explain the changes of these times, and their order arranged and settled by a certain marvelous appointment of Divine Providence.

7. And further, analogy, whereby the agreement of both Testaments is plainly seen, why shall I say that all have made use of, to whose authority they yield; whereas it is in their power to consider with themselves, how many things they are wanting to say have been inserted in the divine Scriptures by certain, I know not who, corrupters of truth? Which speech of theirs I always thought to be most weak, even at the time that I was their hearer: nor I alone, but you also, (for I well remember,) and all of us, who essayed to exercise a little more care in forming a judgment than the crowd of hearers. But now, after that many things have been expounded and made clear to me, which used chiefly to move me: those I mean, wherein their discourse for the most part boasts itself, and

expatiates the more freely, the more safely it can do so as having no opponent; it seems to me that there is no assertion of theirs more shameless, or (to use a milder phrase) more careless and weak than that the divine Scriptures have been corrupted; whereas there are no copies in existence, in a matter of so recent date, whereby they can prove it. For were they to assert, that they thought not that they ought thoroughly to receive them, because they had been written by persons, who they thought had not written the truth; any how their refusal would be more right, or their error more natural. For this is what they have done in the case of the Book which is inscribed the Acts of the Apostles. And this device of theirs, when I consider with myself, I cannot enough wonder at. For it is not the want of wisdom in the men that I complain of in this matter, but the want of ordinary understanding. For that book hath so great matters, which are like what they receive, that it seems to me great folly to refuse to receive this book also, and if anything offend them there to call it false and inserted. Or, if such language is shameless, as it is why in the Epistles of Paul, why in the four books of the Gospel, do they think that they are of any avail, in which I am not sure but that there are in proportion many more things, than could be in that book, which they will have believed to have been interpolated by falsifiers. But forsooth this is what I believe to be the case, and I ask of you to consider it with me with as calm and serene a judgment as possible. For you know that, essaying to bring the person of their founder Manichæus into the number of the Apostles, they say that the Holy Spirit, Whom the Lord promised His disciples that He would send, hath come to us through him. Therefore, were they to receive those Acts of the

Apostles, in which the coming of the Holy Spirit is plainly set forth,1706they could not find how to say that it was interpolated. For they will have it that there were some, I know not who, falsifiers of the divine Books before the times of Manichæus himself; and that they were falsified by persons who wished to combine the Law of the Jews with the Gospel. But this they cannot say concerning the Holy Spirit, unless haply they assert that those persons divined, and set in their books what should be brought forward against Manichæus, who should at some future time arise, and say that the Holy Spirit had been sent through him. But concerning the Holy Spirit we will speak somewhat more plainly in another place. Now let us return to my purpose.

8. For that both history of the Old Testament, and ætiology, and analogy are found in the New Testament, has been, as I think, sufficiently proved: it remains to show this of allegory. Our Redeemer Himself in the Gospel uses allegory out of the Old Testament. "This generation," says He, "seeks a sign, and there shall not be given it save the sign of Jonas the prophet. For as Jonas was three days and three nights in the whale's belly, so also shall the Son of Man be three days and three nights in the heart of the earth." For why should I speak of the Apostle Paul, who in his first Epistle to the Corinthians shows that even the very history of the Exodus was an allegory of the future Christian People. "But I would not that ye should be ignorant, brethren, how that all our fathers were under the cloud, and all passed through the sea, and were all baptized into Moses, in the cloud, and in the sea, and did all eat the same spiritual meat, and did all drink the same spiritual drink; for they drank of the

spiritual Rock that followed with them; and that Rock was Christ. But in the more part of them God was not well pleased: for they were overthrown in the wilderness. But these things were figures of us, that we be not lustful of evil things, as they also lusted. Neither let us worship idols, as certain of them; as it is written, The people sat down to eat and drink, and rose up to play. Neither let us commit fornication, as certain of them committed, and fell in one day three and twenty thousand men. Neither let us tempt Christ, as certain of them tempted, and perished of serpents. Neither murmur we, as certain of them murmured, and perished of the destroyer. But all these things happened unto them in a figure. But they were written for our admonition, upon whom the ends of the world have come." There is also in the Apostle a certain allegory, which indeed greatly relates to the cause in hand, for this reason that they themselves are wanting to bring it forward, and make a display of it in disputing. For the same Paul says to the Galatians, "For it is written, that Abraham had two sons, one of a bond-maid, and one of a free woman. But he who was of the bond-maid was born after the flesh: but he who was of the free woman, by promise: which things were spoken by way of allegory. For these are the two Testaments, one of Mount Sinai gendering unto bondage, which is Agar: for Sinai is a mount in Arabia, which bordered upon that Jerusalem which now is, and is in bondage with her children. But that Jerusalem which is above is free, which is the mother of us all."

9. Here therefore these men too evil, while they essay to make void the Law, force us to approve these Scriptures. For they mark what is said, that they who are

under the Law are in bondage, and they keep flying above the rest that last saying, "Ye are made empty of Christ, as many of you as are justified in the Law; ye have fallen from Grace." We grant that all these things are true, and we say that the Law is not necessary, save for them unto whom bondage is yet profitable: and that the Law was on this account profitably enacted, in that men, who could not be recalled from sins by reason, needed to be restrained by such a Law, that is to say, by the threats and terrors of those punishments which can be seen by fools: from which when the Grace of Christ sets us free, it condemns not that Law, but invites us at length to yield obedience to its love, not to be slaves to the fear of the Law. Itself is Grace, that is free gift, which they understand not to have come to them from God, who still desire to be under the bonds of the Law. Whom Paul deservedly rebukes as unbelievers, because they do not believe that now through our Lord Jesus they have been set free from that bondage, under which they were placed for a certain time by the most just appointment of God. Hence is that saying of the same Apostle, "For the Law was our schoolmaster in Christ." He therefore gave to men a schoolmaster to fear, Who after gave a Master to love. And yet in these precepts and commands of the Law, which now it is not allowed Christians to use, such as either the Sabbath, or Circumcision, or Sacrifices, and if there be any thing of this kind, so great mysteries are contained, as that every pious person may understand, there is nothing deadlier than that whatever is there be understood to the letter, that is, to the word: and nothing more healthful than that it be unveiled in the Spirit. Hence it is: "The letter kills, but the Spirit quickened." Hence it is, "That same veil remained in the reading of the Old

Testament, which veil is not taken away; since it is made void in Christ." For there is made void in Christ, not the Old Testament, but its veil: that so through Christ that may be understood, and, as it were, laid bare, which without Christ is obscure and covered. Forasmuch as the same Apostle straightway adds, "But when thou shalt have passed over to Christ, the veil shall be taken away." For he says not, the Law shall be taken away, or, the Old Testament. Not therefore through the Grace of the Lord, as though useless things were there hidden, have they been taken away; but rather the covering whereby useful things were covered. In this manner all they are dealt with, who earnestly and piously, not disorderly and shamelessly, seek the sense of those Scriptures, and they are carefully shown both the order of events, and the causes of deeds and words, and so great agreement of the Old Testament with the New, that there is left no jot that agrees not; and so great secrets of figures, that all the things that are drawn forth by interpretation force them to confess that they are wretched, who will to condemn these before they learn them.

10. But, passing over in the mean while the depth of knowledge, to deal with you as I think I ought to deal with my intimate friend; that is, as I have myself power, not as I have wondered at the power of very learned men; there are three kinds of error, whereby men err, when they read anything. I will speak of them one by one. The first kind is, wherein that which is false is thought true, whereas the writer thought otherwise. A second kind, although not so extensive, yet not less hurtful, when that, which is false, is thought true, yet the thought is the same as that of the writer. A third kind, when from the writing

of another some truth is understood, whereas the writer understood it not. In which kind there is no little profit, rather, if you consider carefully, the whole entire fruit of reading. An instance of the first kind is, as if anyone, for example, should say and believe that Rhadamanthus hears and judges the causes of the dead in the realms below, because he hath so read in the strain of Maro. For this one errs in two ways: both in that he believes a thing not to be believed, and also in that he, whom he reads, is not to be thought to have believed it. The second kind may be thus noticed: if one, because Lucretius writes that the soul is formed of atoms, and that after death it is dissolved into the same atoms and perishes, were to think this to be true and what he ought to believe. For this one also is not less wretched, if, in a matter of so great moment, he hath persuaded himself of that which is false, as certain; although Lucretius, by whose books he hath been deceived, held this opinion. For what does it profit this one to be assured of the meaning of the author, whereas he hath chosen him to himself not so as through him to escape error, but so as with him to err. An instance suited to the third kind is, if one, after having read in the books of Epicurus some place wherein he praises continence, were to assert that he had made the chief good to consist in virtue, and that therefore he is not to be blamed. For how is this man injured by the error of Epicurus, what though Epicurus believe that bodily pleasure is the chief good of man: whereas he hath not surrendered up himself to so base and hurtful an opinion, and is pleased with Epicurus for no other reason, than that he thinks him not to have held sentiments which ought not to be holden. This error is not only natural to man, but often also most worthy of a man. For what, if word were brought to me, concerning someone whom I loved, that, when now he was of bearded age, he had said, in the hearing of many, that he was so pleased with boyhood and childhood, as even to swear that he wished to live after the same fashion, and that was so proved to me, as that I should be shameless to deny it: I should not, should I, seem worthy of blame, if I thought that, in saying this, he wished to show, that he was pleased with the innocence, and with the temper of mind alien from those desires in which the race of man is wrapped up, and from this circumstance should love him yet more and more, than I used to love him before; although perhaps he had been foolish enough to love in the age of children a certain freedom in play and food, and an idle ease? For suppose that he had died after this report had reached me, and that I had been unable to make any inquiry of him, so as for him to open his meaning; would there be any one so shameless as to be angry with me, for praising the man's purpose and wish, through those very words which I had heard? What, that even a just judge of matters would not hesitate perhaps to praise my sentiment and wish, in that both I was pleased with innocence, and, as man of man, in a matter of doubt, preferred to think well, when it was in my power also to think ill?

11. And, this being so, hear also just so many conditions and differences of the same Scriptures. For it must be that just so many meet us. For either any one hath written profitably, and is not profitably understood by someone: or both take place unprofitably: or the reader understands profitably, whereas he, who is read, hath written contrariwise. Of these the first I blame not, the last I regard not. For neither can I blame the man, who

without any fault of his own hath been ill understood; nor can I be distressed at any one being read, who hath failed to see the truth, when I see that the readers are no way injured. There is then one kind most approved, and as it were most cleansed, when both the things written are well, and are taken in a good sense by the readers. And yet that also is still further divided into two: for it doth not altogether shut out error. For it generally comes to pass, that, when a writer hath held a good sense, the reader also holds a good sense; still other than he, and often better, often worse, yet profitably. But when both we hold the same sense as he whom we read, and that is every way suited to right conduct of life, there is the fullest possible measure of truth, and there is no place opened for error from any other quarter. And this kind is altogether very rare, when what we read is matter of extreme obscurity: nor can it, in my opinion, be clearly known, but only believed. For by what proofs shall I so gather the will of a man who is absent or dead, as that I can swear to it: when, even if he were questioned being present, there might be many things, which, if he were no ill man, he would most carefully hide? But I think that it hath nothing to do towards learning the matter of fact, of what character the writer was; yet is he most fairly believed good, whose writings have benefited the human race and posterity.

12. Wherefore I would that they would tell me, in what kind they place the, supposed, error of the Catholic Church. If in the first, it is altogether a grave charge; but it needs not a far-fetched defense: for it is enough to deny that we so understand, as the persons, who inveigh against us, suppose. If in the second, the charge is not less grave; but they shall be refuted by the same saying. If in the

third, it is no charge at all. Proceed, and next consider the Scriptures themselves. For what objection do they raise against the books of (what is called) the Old Testament? Is it that they are good, but are understood by us in an ill sense? But they themselves do not receive them. Or is it that they are neither good, nor are well understood? But our defense above is enough to drive them from this position. Or is it this that they will say, although they are understood by you in a good sense, yet they are evil? What is this other than to acquit living adversaries, with whom they have to do, and to accuse men long ago dead, with whom they have no strife? I indeed believe that both those men profitably delivered to memory all things, and that they were great and divine. And that that Law was published, and framed by the command and will of God: and of this, although I have but very slight knowledge of books of that kind, yet I can easily persuade any, if there apply to me a mind fair and no way obstinate: and this I will do, when you shall grant to me your ears and mind well disposed: this however when it shall be in my power: but now is it not enough for me, however that matter may stand, not to have been deceived?

13. I call to witness, Honoratus, my conscience, and God Who hath His dwelling in pure souls, that I account nothing more prudent, chaste, and religious, than are all those Scriptures, which under the name of the Old Testament the Catholic Church retains. You wonder at this, I am aware. For I cannot hide that we were far otherwise persuaded. But there is indeed nothing more full of rashness, (which at that time, being boys, we had in us,) than in the case of each several book, to desert expounders, who profess that they hold them, and that

they can deliver them to their scholars, and to seek their meaning from those, who, I know not from what cause compelling, have proclaimed a most bitter war against the framers and authors of them. For whoever thought that the hidden and dark books of Aristotle were to be expounded to him by one who was the enemy of Aristotle; to speak of these systems of teaching, wherein a reader may perhaps err without sacrilege? Who, in fine, willed to read or learn the geometrical writings of Archimedes, under Epicurus as a master; against which Epicurus used to argue with great obstinacy, so far as I judge, understanding them not at all? What are those Scriptures of the law most plain, against which, as though set forth in public, these men make their attack in vain and to no purpose? And they seem to me to be like that weak woman, whom these same men are wont to mock at, who enraged at the sun being extolled to her, and recommended as an object of worship by a certain female Manichee, being as she was simple-minded and of a religions spirit, leaped up in haste, and often striking with her foot that spot on which the sun through the window cast light, began to cry out, Lo, I trample on the sun and your God: altogether after a foolish and womanish manner; Who denies it? But do not those men seem to you to be such, who, in matters which they understand not, either wherefore, or altogether of what kind they are, although like to matters cast in the way, yet to such as understand them exact and divine, rending them with great onset of speech and reproaches, think that they are effecting something, because the unlearned applaud them? Believe me, whatever there is in these Scriptures, it is lofty and divine: there is in them altogether truth, and a system of teaching most suited to refresh and renew minds: and clearly so ordered in measure, as that there is no one but may draw thence, what is enough for himself, if only he approach to draw with devotion and piety, as true religion demands. To prove this to you, needs many reasons and a longer discourse. For first I must so treat with you as that you may not hate the authors themselves; next, so as that you may love them: and this I must treat in any other way, rather than by expounding their meanings and words. For this reason, because in case we hated Virgil, nay, rather in case we loved him not, before understanding him, by the commendation of our forefathers, we should never be satisfied on those questions about him without number, by which grammarians are wanting to be disquieted and troubled; nor should we listen willingly to one who solved these at the same time praising him; but should favor that one who by means of these essayed to show that he had erred and doated. But now, whereas many essay to open these, and each (in a different way according to his capacity, we applaud these in preference, through whose exposition the poet is found better, who is believed, even by those who do not understand him, not only in nothing to have offended, but also to have sung nothing but what was worthy of praise. So that in some minute question, we are rather angry with the master who fails, and has not what to answer, than think him silent through any fault in Maro. And now, if, in order to defend himself, he should wish to assert a fault in so great an author, hardly will his scholars remain with him, even after they have paid his fee. How great matter were it, that we should shew like good will towards them, of whom it hath been confirmed by so long time of old that the Holy Spirit spoke by them? But, forsooth, we youths of the greatest understanding, and marvelous searchers out of reasons, without having at least unrolled these writings, without having sought teachers, without having somewhat chided our own dullness, lastly, without having yielded our heart even in a measure to those who have willed that writings of this kind be so long read, kept, and handled through the whole world; have thought that nothing in them is to be believed, moved by the speech of those who are unfriendly and hostile to them, with whom, under a false promise of reason, we should be compelled to believe and cherish thousands of fables.

14. But now I will proceed with what I have begun, if I can, and I will so treat with you, as not in the mean while to lay open the Catholic Faith, but, in order that they may search out its great mysteries, to show to those who have a care for their souls, hope of divine fruit, and of the discerning of truth. No one doubts of him who seeks true religion, either that he already believes that there is an immortal soul for that religion to profit, or that he also wishes to find that very thing in this same religion. Therefore all religion is for the sake of the soul; for howsoever the nature of the body may be, it causes no care or anxiety, especially after death, to him, whose soul possesses that whereby it is blessed. For the sake of the soul, therefore, either alone or chiefly, hath true religion, if there be any such, been appointed. But this soul, (I will consider for what reason, and I confess the matter to be most obscure,) yet errs, and is foolish, as we see, until it attain to and perceive wisdom, and perhaps this very [wisdom] is true religion. I am not, am I, sending you to fables? I am not, am I, forcing you to believe rashly? I say that our soul entangled and sunk in error and folly seeks

the way of truth, if there be any such. If this be not your case, pardon me, I pray, and share with me your wisdom; but if you recognize in yourself what I say, let us, I entreat, together seek the truth.

15. Put the case that we have not as yet heard a teacher of any religion. Lo we have undertaken a new matter and business. We must seek, I suppose, them who profess this matter, if it have any existence. Suppose that we have found different persons holding different opinions, and through their difference of opinions seeking to draw persons each one to himself: but that, in the meanwhile, there are certain pre-eminent from being much spoken of, and from having possession of nearly all peoples. Whether these hold the truth, is a great question: but ought we not to make full trial of them first, in order that, so long as we err, being as we are men, we may seem to err with the human race itself?

16. But it will be said, the truth is with some few; therefore you already know what it is, if you know with whom it is. Said I not a little above, that we were in search of it as unlearned men? But if from the very force of truth you conjecture that few possess it, but know not who they are; what if it is thus, that there are so few who know the truth, as that they hold the multitude by their authority, whence the small number may set itself free, and, as it were, strain itself forth into those secrets? Do we not see how few attain the highest eloquence, whereas through the whole world the schools of rhetoricians are resounding with troops of young men? What, do they, as many as desire to turn out good orators, alarmed at the multitude of the unlearned, think that they are to bestow

their labor on the orations of Cæcilius, or Erucius, rather than those of Tullius? All aim at these, which are confirmed by authority of our forefathers. Crowds of unlearned persons essay to learn the same, which by the few learned are received as to be learned: yet very few attain, yet fewer practice, the very fewest possible become famous. What, if true religion be some such thing? What if a multitude of unlearned persons attend the Churches, and yet that be no proof, that therefore no one is made perfect by these mysteries? And yet, if they who studied eloquence were as few as the few who are eloquent, our parents would never believe that we ought to be committed to such masters. Whereas, then, we have been called to these studies by a multitude, which is numerous in that portion of it which is made up of the unlearned, so as to become enamored of that which few can attain unto; why are we unwilling to be in the same case in religion, which perhaps we despise with great danger to our soul? For if the truest and purest worship of God, although it be found with a few, be yet found with those, with whom a multitude albeit wrapped up in lusts, and removed far from purity of understanding, agrees; (and who can doubt that this may happen?) I ask, if one were to charge us with rashness and folly, that we seek not diligently with them who teach it, that, which we are greatly anxious to discover, what can we answer? [Shall we say,] I was deterred by numbers? Why from the pursuit of liberal arts, which hardly bring any profit to this present life; why from search after money? Why from attaining unto honor; why, in fine, from gaining and keeping good health; lastly, why from the very aim at a happy life; whereas all are engaged in these, few excel; were you deterred by no numbers?

17. "But they seemed there to make absurd statements." On whose assertion? Forsooth on that of enemies, for whatever cause, for whatever reason, for this is not now the question, still enemies. Upon reading, I found it so of myself. Is it so? Without having received any instruction in poetry, you would not dare to essay to read Terentianus Maurus without a master: Asper, Cornutus, Donatus, and others without number are needed, that any poet whatever may be understood, whose strains seem to court even the applause of the theatre; do you in the case of those books, which, however they may be, yet by the confession of well-nigh the whole human race are commonly reported to be sacred and full of divine things, rush upon them without a guide, and dare to deliver an opinion on them without a teacher; and, if there meet you any matters, which seem absurd, do not accuse rather your own dullness, and mind decayed by the corruption of this world, such as is that of all that are foolish, than those [books] which haply cannot be understood by such persons! You should seek someone at once pious and learned, or who by consent of many was said to be such, that you might be both bettered by his advice, and instructed by his learning. Was he not easy to find? He should be searched out with pains. Was there no one in the country in which you lived? What cause could more profitably force to travel? Was he quite hidden, or did he not exist on the continent? One should cross the sea. If across the sea he was not found in any place near to us, you should proceed even as far as those lands, in which the things related in those books are said to have taken place. What, Honoratus, have we done of this kind? And yet a religion perhaps the most holy, (for as yet I am

speaking as though it were matter of doubt,) the opinion whereof hath by this time taken possession of the whole world, we wretched boys condemned at our own discretion and sentence. What if those things which in those same Scriptures seem to offend some unlearned persons, were so set there for this purpose, that when things were read of such as are abhorrent from the feeling of ordinary men, not to say of wise and holy men, we might with much more earnestness seek the hidden meaning. Perceive you not how the Catamite of the Bucolics, for whom the rough shepherd gushed forth into tears, men essay to interpret, and affirm that the boy Alexis, on whom Plato also is said to have composed a love strain, hath some great meaning or other, but escapes the judgment of the unlearned; whereas without any sacrilege a poet however rich may seem to have published wanton songs?

18. But in truth was there either decree of any law, or power of gainsayers, or vile character of persons consecrated, or shameful report, or newness of institution, or hidden profession, to recall us from, and forbid us, the search? There is nothing of these. All laws divine and human allow us to seek the Catholic Faith; but to hold and exercise it is allowed us at any rate by human law, even if so long as we are in error there be a doubt concerning divine law; no enemy alarms our weakness, (although truth and the salvation of the soul, in case being diligently sought it be not found where it may with most safety, ought to be sought at any risk); the degrees of all ranks and powers most devotedly minister to this divine worship; the name of religion is most honorable and most famous. What, I pray, hinders to search out and discuss

with pious and careful enquiry, whether there be here that which it must needs be few know and guard in entire purity, although the goodwill and affection of all nations conspire in its favor?

19. The case standing thus, suppose, as I said, that we are now for the first time seeking unto what religion we shall deliver up our souls, for it to cleanse and renew them; without doubt we must begin with the Catholic Church. For by this time there are more Christians, than if the Jews and idolaters be added together. But of these same Christians, whereas there are several heresies, and all wish to appear Catholics, and call all others besides themselves heretics, there is one Church, as all allow: if you consider the whole world, more full filled in number; but, as they who know affirm, purer also in truth than all the rest. But the question of truth is another; but, what is enough for such as are in search, there is one Catholic, to which different heresies give different names whereas they themselves are called each by names of their own, which they dare not deny. From which may be understood, by judgment of umpires who are hindered by no favor, to which is to be assigned the name Catholic, which all covet. But, that no one may suppose that it is to be made matter of over garrulous or unnecessary discussion, this is at any rate one, in which human laws themselves also are in a certain way Christian. I do not wish any prejudgment to be formed from this fact, but I account it a most favorable commencement for enquiry. For we are not to fear lest the true worship of God; resting on no strength of its own, seem to need to be supported by them whom it ought to support: but, at any rate, it is perfect happiness, if the truth may be there found, where

it is most safe both to search for it and to hold it: in case it cannot, then at length, at whatever risk, we must go and search some other where.

20. Having then laid down these principles, which, as I think, are so just that I ought to win this cause before you, let who will be my adversary, I will set forth to you, as I am able, what way I followed, when I was searching after true religion in that spirit, in which I have now set forth that it ought to be sought. For upon leaving you and crossing the sea, now delaying and hesitating, what I ought to hold, what to let go; which delay rose upon me every day the more, from the time that I was a hearer of that man, whose coming was promised to us, as you know, as if from heaven, to explain all things which moved us, and found him, with the exception of a certain eloquence, such as the rest; being now settled in Italy, I reasoned and deliberated greatly with myself, not whether I should continue in that sect, into which I was sorry that I had fallen, but in what way I was to find the truth, my sighs through love of which are known to no one better than to yourself. Often it seemed to me that it could not be found, and huge waves of my thoughts would roll toward deciding in favor of the Academics. Often again, with what power I had, looking into the human soul, with so much life, with so much intelligence, with so much clearness, I thought that the truth lay not hid, save that in it the way of search lay hid, and that this same way must be taken from some divine authority. It remained to enquire what was that authority, where in so great dissensions each promised that he would deliver it. Thus there met me a wood, out of which there was no way, which I was very loath to be involved in: and amid these

things, without any rest, my mind was agitated through desire of finding the truth. However, I continued to unsew myself more and more from those whom now I had proposed to leave. But there remained nothing else, in so great dangers, than with words full of tears and sorrow to entreat the Divine Providence to help me. And this I was content to do: and now certain disputations of the Bishop of Milan had almost moved me to desire, not without some hope, to enquire into many things concerning the Old Testament itself, which, as you know, we used to view as accursed, having been ill commended to us. And I had decided to be a Catechumen in the Church, unto which I had been delivered by my parents, until such time as I should either find what I wished, or should persuade myself that it needed not to be sought. Therefore had there been one who could teach me, he would find me at a very critical moment most fervently disposed and very apt to learn. If you see that you too have been long affected in this way, therefore, and with a like care for thy soul, and if now you seem to yourself to have been tossed to and fro enough, and wish to put an end to labors of this kind, follow the pathway of Catholic teaching, which hath flowed down from Christ Himself through the Apostles even unto us, and will hereafter flow down to posterity.

21. This, you will say, is ridiculous, whereas all profess to hold and teach this: all heretics make this profession, I cannot deny it; but so, as that they promise to those whom they entice, that they will give them a reason concerning matters the most obscure: and on this account chiefly charge the Catholic [Church], that they who come to her are enjoined to believe; but they make it their boast, that they impose not a yoke of believing, but

open a fount of teaching. You answer, What could be said, that should pertain more to their praise? It is not so. For this they do, without being endued with any strength, but in order to conciliate to themselves a crowd by the name of reason: on the promise of which the human soul naturally is pleased, and, without considering its own strength and state of health, by seeking the food of the sound, which is ill entrusted save to such as are in health, rushes upon the poisons of them who deceive. For true religion, unless those things be believed, which each one after, if he shall conduct himself well and shall be worthy, attains unto and understands, and altogether without a certain weighty power of authority, can in no way be rightly entered upon.

22. But perhaps you seek to have some reason given you on this very point, such as may persuade you, that you ought not to be taught by reason before faith. Which may easily be done, if only you make yourself a fair hearer. But, in order that it may be done suitably, I wish you as it were to answer my questions; and, first, to tell me, why you, think that one ought not to believe. Because, you say, credulity, from which men are called credulous, in itself, seems to me to be a certain fault: otherwise we should not use to cast this as a term of reproach. For if a suspicious man is in fault, in that he suspects things not ascertained; how much more a credulous man, who herein differs from a suspicious man, that the one allows some doubt, the other none, in matters which he knows not. In the mean while I accept this opinion and distinction. But you know that we are not wont to call a person even curious without some reproach; but we call him studious even with praise. Wherefore

observe, if you please, what seems to you to be the difference between these two. This surely, you answer, that, although both be led by great desire to know, yet the curious man seeks after things that no way pertain to him, but the studious man, on the contrary, seeks after what pertain to him. But, because we deny not that a man's wife and children, and their health, pertain unto him; if anyone, being settled abroad, were to be careful to ask all comers, how his wife and children are and fare, he is surely led by great desire to know, and yet we call not this man studious, who both exceedingly wishes to know, and that (in) matters which very greatly pertain unto him. Wherefore you now understand that the definition of a studious person falters in this point, that every studious person wishes to know what pertain to himself, and yet not everyone, who makes this his business, is to be called studious; but he who with all earnestness seeks those things which pertain unto the liberal culture and adornment of the mind. Yet we rightly call him one who studies, especially if we add what he studies to hear. For we may call him even studious of his own (family) if he love only his own (family), we do not however, without some addition, think him worthy of the common name of the studious. But one who was desirous to hear how his family were I should not call studious of hearing, unless taking pleasure in the good report, he should wish to hear it again and again: but one who studied, even if only once. Now return to the curious person, and tell me, if anyone should be willing to listen to some tale, such as would no way profit him, that is, of matters that pertain not to him: and that not in an offensive way and frequently, but very seldom and with great moderation, either at a feast, or in some company, or meeting of any kind; would he seem to you curious? I think not: but at any rate he would certainly seem to have a care for that matter, to which he was willing to listen. Wherefore the definition of a curious person also must be corrected by the same rule as that of a studious person: Consider therefore whether the former statements also do not need to be corrected. For why should not both he, who at some time suspects something, be unworthy the name of a suspicious person; and he who at some time believes something, of a credulous person? Thus as there is very great difference between one who studies any matter, and the absolutely studious; and again between him who hath a care and the curious; so is there between him who believes and the credulous.

23. But you will say, consider now whether we ought to believe in religion. For, although we grant that it is one thing to believe, another to be credulous, it does not follow that it is no fault to believe in matters of religion. For what if it be a fault both to believe and to be credulous, as (it is) both to be drunk and to be a drunkard? Now he who thinks this certain, it seems to me can have no friend; for, if it is base to believe anything, either he acts basely who believes a friend, or in nothing believing a friend I see not how he can call either him or himself a friend. Here perhaps you may say, I grant that we must believe something at some time; now make plain, how in the case of religion it be not base to believe before one knows. I will do so, if I can. Wherefore I ask of you, which you esteem the graver fault, to deliver religion to one unworthy, or to believe what is said by them who deliver it. If you understand not whom I call unworthy, I call him, who approaches with feigned breast. You grant,

as I suppose, that it is more blamable to unfold unto such an one whatever holy secrets there are, than to believe religious men affirming anything on the matter of religion itself. For it would be unbecoming you to make any other answer. Wherefore now suppose him present, who is about to deliver to you a religion, in what way shall you assure him, that you approach with a true mind, and that, so far as this matter is concerned, there is in you no fraud or feigning? You will say, your own good conscience that you are no way feigning, asserting this with words as strong as you can, but yet with words. For you cannot lay open man to man the hiding places of your soul, so that you may be thoroughly known. But if he shall say, Lo, I believe you, but is it not fairer that you also believe me, when, if I hold any truth, you are about to receive, I about to give, a benefit? what will you answer, save that you must believe.

24. But you say, Were it not better that you should give me a reason, that, wherever, that shall lead me, I may follow without any rashness? Perhaps it were: but, it being so great a matter, that you are by reason to come to the knowledge of God, do you think that all are qualified to understand the reasons, by which the human soul is led to know God, or many, or few? Few I think, you say. Do you believe that you are in the number of these? It is not for me, you say, to answer this. Therefore you think it is for him to believe you in this also: and this indeed he does: only do you remember, that he hath already twice believed you saying things uncertain; that you are unwilling to believe him even once admonishing you in a religious spirit. But suppose that it is so, and that you approach with a true mind to receive religion, and that

you are one of few men in such sense as to be able to take in the reasons by which the Divine Power1734 is brought into certain knowledge; what? do you think that other men, who are not endued with so serene a disposition, are to be denied religion? or do you think that they are to be led gradually by certain steps unto those highest inner recesses? You see clearly which is the more religious. For you cannot think that anyone whatever in a case where he desires so great a thing, ought by any means to be abandoned or rejected. But do you not think, that, unless he do first believe that he shall attain unto that which he purposes; and do yield his mind as a suppliant; and, submitting to certain great and necessary precepts, do by a certain course of life thoroughly cleanse it, that he will not otherwise attain the things that are purely true? Certainly you think so. What, then, is the case of those, (of whom I already believe you to be one,) who are able most easily to receive divine secrets by sure reason, will it, I ask, be to them any hindrance at all, if they so come as they who at the first believe? I think not. But yet, you say, what need to delay them? Because although they will in no way harm themselves by what is done, yet they will harm the rest by the precedent. For there is hardly one who has a just notion of his own power: but he who has a less notion must be roused; he who has a greater notion must be checked: that neither the one be broken by despair, nor the other carried headlong by rashness. And this is easily done, if even they, who are able to fly, (that they be not alluring the occasion of any into danger,) are forced for a short time to walk where the rest also may walk with safety. This is the forethought of true religion: this the command of God: this what hath been handed down from our blessed forefathers, this what hath been preserved even unto us: to wish to distrust and overthrow this, is nothing else than to seek a sacrilegious way unto true religion. And whoso do this, not even if what they wish be granted to them are they able to arrive at the point at which they aim. For whatever kind of excellent genius they have, unless God be present, they creep on the ground. But He is then present, if they, who are aiming at God, have a regard for their fellow men. Than which step there can be found nothing more sure Heavenward. I for my part cannot resist this reasoning, for how can I say that we are to believe nothing without certain knowledge? whereas both there can be no friendship at all, unless there be believed something which cannot be proved by some reason, and often stewards, who are slaves, are trusted by their masters without any fault on their part. But in religion what can there be more unfair than that the ministers of God believe us when we promise an unfeigned mind, and we are unwilling to believe them when they enjoin us anything. Lastly, what way can there be more healthful, than for a man to become fitted to receive the truth by believing those things, which have been appointed by God to serve for the previous culture and treatment of the mind? Or, if you be already altogether fitted, rather to make some little circuit where it is safest to tread, than both to cause yourself danger, and to be a precedent for rashness to other men?

25. Wherefore it now remains to consider, in what manner we ought not to follow these, who profess that they will lead by reason. For how we may without fault follow those who bid us to believe, hath been already said: but unto these who make promises of reason certain think that they come, not only without blame, but also

with some praise: but it is not so. For there are two (classes of) persons, praiseworthy in religion; one of those who have already found, whom also we must needs judge most blessed; another of those who are seeking with all earnestness and in the right way. The first, therefore, are already in very possession, the other on the way, yet on that way whereby they are most sure to arrive. There are three other kinds of men altogether to be disapproved of and detested. One is of those who hold an opinion, that is, of those who think that they know what they know not. Another is of those who are indeed aware that they know not, but do not so seek as to be able to find. A third is of those who neither think that they know, nor wish to seek. There are also three things, as it were bordering upon one another, in the minds of men well worth distinguishing; understanding, belief, opinion. And, if these be considered by themselves, the first is always without fault, the second sometimes with fault, the third never without fault. For the understanding of matters great, and honorable, and even divine, is most blessed. But the understanding of things unnecessary is no injury; but perhaps the learning was an injury, in that it took up the time of necessary matters. But on the matters themselves that are injurious, it is not the understanding, but the doing or suffering them, that is wretched. For not, in case any understand how an enemy may be slain without danger to himself, is he guilty from the mere understanding, not the wish; and, if the wish be absent, what can be called more innocent? But belief is then worthy of blame, when either anything is believed of God which is unworthy of Him, or anything is over easily believed of man. But in all other matters if any believe aught, provided he understand that he knows it not, there is no fault. For I believe that very wicked conspirators were formerly put to death by the virtue of Cicero; but this I not only know not, but also I know for certain that I can by no means know. But opinion is on two accounts very base; in that both he who hath persuaded himself that he already knows, cannot learn; provided only it may be learnt; and in itself rashness is a sign of a mind not well disposed. For even if any suppose that he know what I said of Cicero, (although it be no hindrance to him from learning, in that the matter itself is incapable of being grasped by any knowledge;) yet, (in that he understands not that there is a great difference, whether anything be grasped by sure reason of mind, which we call understanding, or whether for practical purposes it be entrusted to common fame or writing, for posterity to believe it,) he assuredly errs, and no error is without what is base. What then we understand, we owe to reason; what we believe, to authority; what we have an opinion on, to error. But everyone who understands also believes, and also everyone who has an opinion believes; not everyone who believes understands, no one who has an opinion understands. Therefore if these three things be referred unto the five kinds of men, which we mentioned a little above; that is, two kinds to be approved, which we set first, and three that remain faulty; we find that the first kind, that of the blessed, believe the truth itself; but the second kind, that of such as are earnest after, and lovers of, the truth, believe authority. In which kinds, of the two, the act of belief is praiseworthy. But in the first of the faulty kinds, that is, of those who have an opinion that they know what they know not, there is an altogether faulty credulity. The other two kinds that are to be disapproved believe nothing, both they who seek the truth despairing of finding it, and they who seek it not at all. And this only in matters which pertain unto any system of teaching. For in the other business of life, I am utterly ignorant by what means a man can believe nothing. Although in the case of those also they who say that in practical matters they follow probabilities, would seem rather to be unable to know than unable to believe. For who believes not what he approves? or how is what they follow probable, if it be not approved? Wherefore there may be two kinds of such as oppose the truth: one of those who assail knowledge alone, not faith; the other of those who condemn both: and yet again, I am ignorant whether these can be found in matters of human life. These things have been said, in order that we might understand, that, in retaining faith, even of those things which as yet we comprehend not, we are set free from the rashness of such as have an opinion. For they, who say that we are to believe nothing but what we know, are on their guard against that one name "opining," which must be confessed to be base and very wretched, but, if they consider carefully that there is a very great difference, whether one think that he knows, or moved by some authority believe that which he understands that he knows not, surely he will escape the charge of error, and inhumanity, and pride.

26. For I ask, if what is not known must not be believed, in what way may children do service to their parents, and love with mutual affection those whom they believe not to be their parents? For it cannot, by any means, be known by reason. But the authority of the mother comes in, that it be believed of the father; but of the mother it is usually not the mother that is believed, but

midwives, nurses, servants. For she, from whom a son may be stolen and another put in his place, may she not being deceived deceive? Yet we believe, and believe without any doubt, what we confess we cannot know. For who but must see, that unless it be so, filial affection, the most sacred bond of the human race, is violated by extreme pride of wickedness? For what madman even would think him to be blamed who discharged the duties that were due to those whom he believed to be his parents, although they were not so? Who, on the other hand, would not judge him to deserve banishment, who failed to love those who were perhaps his true parents, through fear lest he should love pretended. Many things may be alleged, whereby to show that nothing at all of human society remains safe, if we shall determine to believe nothing, which we cannot grasp by full apprehension.

27. But now hear, what I trust I shall by this time more easily persuade you of. In a matter of religion, that is, of the worship and knowledge of God, they are less to be followed, who forbid us to believe, making most ready professions of reason. For no one doubts that all men are either fools or wise. But now I call wise, not clever and gifted men, but those, in whom there is, so much as may be in man, the knowledge of man himself and of God most surely received, and a life and manners suitable to that knowledge; but all others, whatever be their skill or want of skill, whatever their manner of life, whether to be approved or disapproved, I would account in the number of fools. And, this being so, who of moderate understanding but will clearly see, that it is more useful and more healthful for fools to obey the precepts of the wise, than to live by their own judgment? For everything

that is done, if it be not rightly done, is a sin, nor can that anyhow be rightly done which proceeds not from right reason. Further, right reason is very virtue. But to whom of men is virtue at hand, save to the mind of the wise? Therefore the wise man alone sins not. Therefore every fool sins, save in those actions, in which he hath obeyed a wise man: for all such actions proceed from right reason, and, so to say, the fool is not to be accounted master of his own action, he being, as it were, the instrument and that which ministers to the wise man. Wherefore, if it be better for all men not to sin than to sin; assuredly all fools would live better, if they could be slaves of the wise. And, if no one doubts that this is better in lesser matters, as in buying and selling, and cultivating the ground, in taking a wife, in undertaking and bringing up children, lastly, in the management of household property, much more in religion. For both human matters are more easy to distinguish between, than divine; and in all matters of greater sacredness and excellence, the greater obedience and service we owe them, the more wicked and the more dangerous is it to sin. Therefore you see henceforth that nothing else is left us, so long as we are fools, if our heart be set on an excellent and religious life, but to seek wise men, by obeying whom we may be enabled both to lessen the great feeling of the rule of folly, whilst it is in us, and at the last to escape from it.

28. Here again arises a very difficult question. For in what way shall we fools be able to find a wise man, whereas this name, although hardly anyone dare openly, yet most men lay claim to indirectly: so disagreeing one with another in the very matters, in the knowledge of which wisdom consists, as that it must needs be that either

none of them, or but some certain one be wise? But when the fool enquires, who is that wise man? I do not at all see, in what way he can be distinguished and perceived. For by no signs whatever can one recognize anything, unless he shall have known that thing, whereof these are signs. But the fool is ignorant of wisdom. For not, as, in the case of gold and silver and other things of that kind, it is allowed both to know them when you see them and not to have them, thus may wisdom be seen by the mind's eye of him who hath it not. For whatever things we come into contact with by bodily sense, are presented to us from without; and therefore we may perceive by the eyes what belong to others, when we ourselves possess not any of them or of that kind. But what is perceived by the understanding is within in the mind, and to have it is nothing else than to see. But the fool is void of wisdom, therefore he knows not wisdom. For he could not see it with the eyes: but he cannot see it and not have it, nor have it and be a fool. Therefore he knows it not, and, so long as he knows it not, he cannot recognize it in another place. No one, so long as he is a fool, can by most sure knowledge find out a wise man, by obeying whom he may be set free from so great evil of folly.

29. Therefore this so vast difficulty, since our enquiry is about religion, God alone can remedy: nor indeed, unless we believe both that He is, and that He helps men's minds, ought we even to enquire after true religion itself. For what I ask do we with so great endeavor desire to search out? What do we wish to attain unto? Whither do we long to arrive? Is it at that which we believe not exists or pertains to us? Nothing is more perverse than such a state of mind. Then, when you would

not dare to ask of me a kindness, or at any rate would be shameless in daring, come you to demand the discovery of religion, when you think that God neither exists, nor, if He exist, hath any care for us? What, if it be so great a matter, as that it cannot be found out, unless it be sought carefully and with all our might? What, if the very extreme difficulty of discovery be an exercise for the mind of the inquirer, in order to receive what shall be discovered? For what more pleasant and familiar to our eyes than this light? And yet men are unable after long darkness to hear and endure it. What more suited to the body exhausted by sickness than meat and drink? And yet we see that persons who are recovering are restrained and checked, lest they dare to commit themselves to the fullness of persons in health, and so bring to pass by means of their very food their return to that disease which used to reject it. I speak of persons who are recovering. What, the very sick, do we not urge them to take something? Wherein assuredly they would not with so great discomfort obey us, if they believed not that they would recover from that disease. When then will you give yourself up to a search very full of pains and labor? When will you have the heart to impose upon yourself so great care and trouble as the matter deserves, when you believe not in the existence of that which you are in search of? Rightly therefore hath it been ordained by the majesty of the Catholic system of teaching, that they who approach unto religion be before all things persuaded to have faith.

30. Wherefore that heretic, (inasmuch as our discourse is of those who wish to be called Christians,) I ask you, what reason he alleges to me? What is there whereby for him to call me back from believing, as if

from rashness? If he bid me believe nothing; I believe not that this very true religion hath any existence in human affairs; and what I believe not to exist, I seek not. But He, as I suppose, will show it to me seeking it: for so it written, "He that seeks shall find." Therefore I should not come unto him, who forbids me to believe, unless I believed something. Is there any greater madness, than that I should displease him by faith alone, which is founded on no knowledge, which faith alone led me to him?

31. What, that all heretics exhort us to believe in Christ? Can they possibly be more opposed to themselves? And in this matter they are to be pressed in a twofold way. In the first place we must ask of them, where is the reason which they used to promise, where the reproof of rashness, where the assumption of knowledge? For, if it be disgraceful to believe any without reason, what do you wait for, what are you busied about, that I believe someone without reason, in order that I may the more easily be led by your reason? What, will your reason raise any firm superstructure on the foundation of rashness? I speak after their manner, whom we displease by believing. For I not only judge it most healthful to believe before reason, when you are not qualified to receive reason, and by the very act of faith thoroughly to cultivate the mind to receive the seeds of truth, but altogether a thing of such sort as that without it health cannot return to sick souls. And in that this seems to them matter for mockery and full of rashness, surely they are shameless in making it their business that we believe in Christ. Next, I confess that I have already believed in Christ, and have convinced myself that what He hath said

is true, although it be supported by no reason; is this, heretic, what you will teach me in the first place? Suffer me to consider a little with myself, (since I have not seen Christ Himself, as He willed to appear unto men, Who is said to have been seen by them, even by common eyes,) who they are that I have believed concerning Him, in order that I may approach you already furnished beforehand with such a faith. I see that there are none that I have believed, save the confirmed opinion and widely extended report of peoples and nations: and that the mysteries of the Church Catholic have in all times and places had possession of these peoples. Why therefore shall I not of these, in preference to others, inquire with all care, what Christ commanded, by whose authority I have been moved already to believe that Christ hath commanded something that is profitable? Are you likely to be a better expounder to me of what He said, Whose past or present existence I should not believe, if by you I were to be recommended to believe thus? This therefore I have believed, as I said, trusting to report strengthened by numbers, agreement, antiquity. But you, who are both so few, and so turbulent, and so new, no one doubts that ye bring forward nothing worthy of authority. What then is that so great madness? Believe them, that you are to believe in Christ, and learn from us what He said. Why, I pray you? For were they to fail and to be unable to teach me anything with much greater ease could I persuade myself, that I am not to believe in Christ, than that I am to learn anything concerning Him, save from those through whom I had believed in Him. O vast confidence, or rather absurdity! I teach you what Christ, in Whom you believe, commanded. What, in case I believed not in Him? You could not, could you, teach me anything concerning Him?

But, says he, it behooves you to believe. You do not mean, do you, that I am (to believe) you when you commend Him to my faith? No, says he, for we lead by reason them who believe in Him. Why then should I believe in Him? Because report hath been grounded. Whether is it through you, or through others? Through others, says he. Shall I then believe them, in order that you may teach me? Perhaps I ought to do so, were it not that they gave me this chief charge, that I should not approach you at all; for they say that you have deadly doctrines. You will answer, They lie. How then shall I believe them concerning Christ, Whom they have not seen, (and) not believe them concerning you, whom they are unwilling to see? Believe the Scriptures, says he. But every writing, if it be brought forward new and unheard of, or be commended by few, with no reason to confirm it, it is not it that is believed, but they who bring it forward. Wherefore, for those Scriptures, if you are they who bring them forward, you so few and unknown, I am not pleased to believe them. At the same time also you are acting contrary to your promise, in enforcing faith rather than giving a reason. You will recall me again to numbers and (common) report. Curb, I pray you, your obstinacy, and that untamed lust, I know not what, of spreading your name: and advise me rather to seek the chief men of this multitude, and to seek with all care and pains rather to learn something concerning these writings from these men, but for whose existence, I should not know that I had to learn at all. But do you return into your dens, and lay not any snares under the name of truth, which you endeavor to take from those, to whom you yourself grant authority.

32. But if they say that we are not even to believe in Christ, unless undoubted reason shall be given us, they are not Christians. For this is what certain pagans say against us, foolishly indeed, yet not contrary to, or inconsistent with, themselves. But who can endure that these profess to belong to Christ, who contend that they are to believe nothing, unless they shall bring forward to fools most open reason concerning God? But we see that He Himself, so far as that history, which they themselves believe, teaches, willed nothing before, or more strongly than, that He should be believed in: whereas they, with whom He had to do, were not yet qualified to receive the secret things of God. For, for what other purpose are so great and so many miracles, He Himself also saying, that they are done for no other cause, than that He may be believed in? He used to lead fools by faith, you lead by reason. He used to cry out, that He should be believed in, ye cry out against it. He used to praise such as believe in Him, ye blame them. But unless either He should change water into wine, to omit other (miracles), if men would follow Him, doing no such, but (only) teaching; either we must make no account of that saying, "Believe ye God, believe also Me;" or we must charge him with rashness, who willed not that He should come into his house, believing that the disease of his servant would depart at His mere command. Therefore He bringing to us a medicine such as should heal our utterly corrupt manners, by miracles procured to Himself authority, by authority obtained Himself belief, by belief drew together a multitude, by a multitude possessed antiquity, by antiquity strengthened religion: so that not only the utterly foolish novelty of heretics dealing deceitfully, but also the inveterate error of the nations opposing with violence,

On the Profit of Believing

should be unable on any side to rend it asunder.

33. Wherefore, although I am not able to teach, yet I cease not to advise, that, (whereas many wish to appear wise, and it is no easy matter to discern whether they be fools,) with all earnestness, and with all prayers, and lastly with groans, or even, if so it may be, with tears, you entreat of God to set you free from the evil of error; if your heart be set on a happy life. And this will take place the more easily, if you obey with a willing mind His commands, which He hath willed should be confirmed by so great authority of the Catholic Church. For whereas the wise man is so joined to God in mind, as that there is nothing set between to separate; for God is Truth; and no one is by any means wise, unless his mind encounter the Truth; we cannot deny that between the folly of man, and the purest Truth of God, the wisdom of man is set, as something in the middle. For the wise man, so far as it is given unto him, imitates God; but for a man who is a fool, there is nothing nearer to him, than a man who is wise, for him to imitate with profit: and since, as has been said, it is not easy to understand this one by reason, it behooved that certain miracles be brought near to the very eyes, which fools use with much greater readiness than the mind, that, men being moved by authority, their life and habits might first be cleansed, and they thus rendered capable of receiving reason. Whereas, therefore, it needed both that man be imitated, and that our hope be not set in man, what could be done on the part of God more full of kindness and grace, than that the very pure, eternal, unchangeable Wisdom of God, unto Whom it behooves us to cleave, should deign to take upon Him (the nature of) man? That not only He might do what should invite us

to follow God, but also might suffer what used to deter us from following God. For, whereas no one can attain unto the most sure and chief good, unless he shall fully and perfectly love it; which will by no means take place, so long as the evils of the body and of fortune are dreaded; He by being born after a miraculous manner and working caused Himself to be loved; and by dying and rising again shut out fear. And, further, in all other matters, which it were long to go through, He shewed Himself such, as that we might perceive unto what the clemency of God could be reached forth, and unto what the weakness of man be lifted up.

34. This is, believe me, a most wholesome authority, this a lifting up first of our mind from dwelling on the earth, this a turning from the love of this world unto the True God. It is authority alone which moves fools to hasten unto wisdom. So long as we cannot understand pure (truths), it is indeed wretched to be deceived by authority, but surely more wretched not to be moved. For, if the Providence of God preside not over human affairs, we have no need to busy ourselves about religion. But if both the outward form of all things, which we must believe assuredly flows from some fountain of truest beauty, and some, I know not what, inward conscience exhorts, as it were, in public and in private, all the better order of minds to seek God, and to serve God; we must not give up all hope that the same God Himself hath appointed some authority, whereon, resting as on a sure step, we may be lifted up unto God. But this, setting aside reason, which (as we have often said) it is very hard for fools to understand pure, moves us two ways; in part by miracles, in part by multitude of followers: no one of

these is necessary to the wise man; who denies it? But this is now the business in hand, that we may be able to be wise, that is, to cleave to the truth; which the filthy soul is utterly unable to do: but the filth of the soul, to say shortly what I mean, is the love of any things whatsoever save God and the soul: from which filth the more anyone is cleansed, the more easily he sees the truth. Therefore to wish to see the truth, in order to purge your soul, when as it is purged for the very purpose that you may see, is surely perverse and preposterous. Therefore to man unable to see the truth, authority is at hand, in order that he may be made fitted for it, and may allow himself to be cleansed; and, as I said a little above, no one doubts that this prevails, in part by miracles, in part by multitude. But I call that a miracle, whatever appears that is difficult or unusual above the hope or power of them who wonder. Of which kind there is nothing more suited for the people, and in general for foolish men, than what is brought near to the senses. But these, again, are divided into two kinds; for there are certain, which cause only wonder, but certain others procure also great favor and good-will. For, if one were to see a man flying, inasmuch as that matter brings no advantage to the spectator, beside the spectacle itself, he only wonders. But if any affected with grievous and hopeless disease were to recover straightway, upon being bidden, his affection for him who heals, will go beyond even his wonder at his healing. Such were done at that time at which God in True Man appeared unto men, as much as was enough. The sick were healed, the lepers were cleansed; walking was restored to the lame, sight to the blind, hearing to the deaf. The men of that time saw water turned into wine, five thousand filled with five loaves, seas passed on foot, dead rising again: thus certain provided for the good of the body by more open benefit, certain again for the good of the soul by more hidden sign, and all for the good of men by their witness to Majesty: thus, at that time, was the divine authority moving towards Itself the wandering souls of mortal men. Why, say you, do not those things take place now? because they would not move, unless they were wonderful, and, if they were usual, they would not be wonderful. For the interchanges of day and night, and the settled order of things in Heaven, the revolution of years divided into four parts, the fall and return of leaves to trees, the boundless power of seeds, the beauty of light, the varieties of colors, sounds, tastes, and scents, let there be someone who shall see and perceive them for the first time, and yet such an one as we may converse with; he is stupefied and overwhelmed with miracles: but we condemn all these, not because they are easy to understand, (for what more obscure than the causes of these?) but surely because they constantly meet our senses. Therefore they were done at a very suitable time, in order that, by these a multitude of believers having been gathered together and spread abroad, authority might be turned with effect upon habits.

35. But any habits whatever have so great power to hold possession of men's minds, that even what in them are evil, which usually takes place through excess of lusts, we can sooner disapprove of and hate, than desert or change. Do you think that little hath been done for the benefit of man, that not some few very learned men maintain by argument, but also an unlearned crowd of males and females in so many and different nations both believe and set forth, that we are to worship as God

nothing of earth, nothing of fire, nothing, lastly, which comes into contact with the senses of the body, but that we are to seek to approach Him by the understanding only? that abstinence is extended even unto the slenderest food of bread and water, and fastings not only for the day, but also continued through several days together; that chastity is carried even unto the contempt of marriage and family; that patience even unto the setting light by crosses and flames; that liberality even unto the distribution of estates unto the poor; that, lastly, the contempt of this whole world even unto the desire of death? Few do these things, yet fewer do them well and wisely: but whole nations approve, nations hear, nations favor, nations, lastly, love. Nations accuse their own weakness that they cannot do these things, and that not without the mind being carried forward unto God, nor without certain sparks of virtue. This hath been brought to pass by the Divine Providence, through the prophecies of the Prophets, through the manhood and teaching of Christ, through the journeys of the Apostles, through the insults, crosses, blood, of the Martyrs, through the praiseworthy life of the Saints, and, in all these, according as times were seasonable, through miracles worthy of so great matters and virtues. When therefore we see so great help of God, so great progress and fruit, shall we doubt to hide ourselves in the bosom of that Church, which even unto the confession of the human race from [the] apostolic chair through successions of Bishops, (heretics in vain lurking around her and being condemned, partly by the judgment of the very people, partly by the weight of councils, partly also by the majesty of miracles,) hath held the summit of authority. To be unwilling to grant to her the first place, is either surely the height of impiety, or is headlong arrogance. For, if there be no sure way unto wisdom and health of souls, unless where faith prepare them for reason, what else is it to be ungrateful for the Divine help and aid, than to wish to resist authority furnished with so great labor? And if every system of teaching, however mean and easy, requires, in order to its being received, a teacher or master, what more full of rash pride, than, in the case of books of divine mysteries, both to be unwilling to learn from such as interpret them, and to wish to condemn them unlearned?

36. Wherefore, if either our reasoning or our discourse hath in any way moved you, and if you have, as I believe, a true care for yourself, I would you would listen to me, and with pious faith, lively hope, and simple charity, entrust yourself to good teachers of Catholic Christianity; and cease not to pray unto God Himself, by Whose goodness alone we were created, and suffer punishment by His justice, and are set free by His mercy. Thus there will be wanting to you neither precepts and treatises of most learned and truly Christian men, nor books, nor calm thoughts themselves, whereby you may easily find what you are seeking. For do you abandon utterly those wordy and wretched men, (for what other milder name can I use?) who, whilst they seek to excess whence is evil, find nothing but evil. And on this question they often rouse their hearers to inquire; but after that they have been roused, they teach them such lessons as that it were preferable even to sleep forever, than than thus to be awake. For in place of lethargic they make them frantic, between which diseases, both being usually fatal, there is still this difference, that lethargic persons die without doing violence to others; but the frantic person many who

are sound, and specially they who wish to help him, have reason to fear. For neither is God the author of evil, nor hath it ever repented Him that He hath done aught, nor is He troubled by storm of any passion of soul, nor is a small part of earth His Kingdom: He neither approves nor commands any sins or wickedness, He never lies. For these and such like used to move us, when they used them to make great and threatening assaults, and charged this as being the system of teaching of the Old Testament, which is most false. Thus then I allow that they do right in censuring these. What then have I learnt? What think you, save that, when these are censured, the Catholic system of teaching is not censured. Thus what I had learnt among them that is true, I hold, what is false that I had thought I reject. But the Catholic Church hath taught me many other things also, which those men of bloodless bodies, but coarse minds, cannot aspire unto; that is to say, that God is not corporeal, that no part of Him can be perceived by corporeal eyes, that nothing of His Substance or Nature can any way suffer violence or change, or is compounded or formed; and if you grant me these, (for we may not think otherwise concerning God,) all their devices are overthrown. But how it is, that neither God begot or created evil, nor yet is there, or hath there been ever, any nature and substance, which God either begot not or created not, and yet that He sets us free from evil, is proved by reasons so necessary, that it cannot at all be matter of doubt; especially to you and such as you; that is, if to a good disposition there be added piety and a certain peace of mind, without which nothing at all can be understood concerning so great matters. And here there is no rumor concerning smoke, and I know not what Persian vain fable, unto which it is enough to lend an ear, and soul not subtile, but absolutely childish. Far altogether, far otherwise is the truth, than as the Manichees dote. But since this discourse of ours hath gone much further than I thought, here let us end the book; in which I wish you to remember, that I have not yet begun to refute the Manichees, and that I have not yet assailed that nonsense; and that neither have I unfolded anything great concerning the Catholic Church itself, but that I have only wished to root out of you, if I could, a false notion concerning true Christians that was maliciously or ignorantly suggested to us, and to arouse you to learn certain great and divine things. Wherefore let this volume be as it is; but when your soul becomes more calmed, I shall perhaps be more ready in what remains.